Abstract Visions of Light

Scott Thomas Outlar

Alien Buddha Press 2018

Abstract Visions of Light
First Edition

Published by Alien Buddha Press

ISBN-13: 978-1984155917
ISBN-10: 1984155911

Printed in the United States of America

Front cover art: Red Focks

Back cover photograph: Mechelle Wilson Ballew

Interior photography: Red Focks

This book is dedicated to all of the women who have helped shape my life in a positive fashion. My mother, my sister, my grandmothers, my aunts, my nieces, my cousins, and my friends.

To Michael —
Hope you have a happy holiday
season, my friend, and cheers to a
great 2019 ahead! Thank you for
being such a gracious host at Phoenix
and Oregon each month.

Selah,
[signature]
12/14/2018

Preface

I had a pretty toasty sleeping bag, notwithstanding the frozen ground and broken zipper. Awoken by whizzing and gusts of wind from the sporadic traffic. I rise up with love in my heart. I'm forty miles from Slab City, averaging one hundred a day. I got dropped off in the middle of nowhere by a Mexican big rig driver, the night prior.

People who pick up hitchhikers are funny. Half of them tell me that I just don't look like a person who'd murder them. I want to tell them it's always the ones you'd least expect, but obviously I don't. An old man with a pickup truck tells me I can hop in the bed. The cold desert air opens eyes wider than ten cups of coffee

I meet two hippies with their thumbs out. They tell me Slab City's just down the road behind us. I trade them some cigarettes and a copy of my book for some grass and a copy of *Into the Wild*. One of the hippies tells me, "This book man... This book will make you want to... like... go i n t o the w i l d."

I make my way down that dirt road. I find a 7 of spades playing card, and I wear the symbolism with pride in the brim of my hat. The first car I see tells me to "cram in." I don't even need to put my thumb out because they already know where I'm going. They're taking me to "The Last Free City in America."

Just over a year later, I am ecstatic that the photos I took on that day are now the illustrations for *Abstract Visions of Light* by Scott Thomas Outlar. This follow-up to our 2017 collaboration, *Poison in Paradise*, is the ideal piece to pair the artistic phenomena that is Slab City.

-Red Focks, Alien Buddha Press 2018

Table of Contents

Transcending Definitions

Art is not an institution…
it is an inner fire
born out of those
whose eyes pierce deeply
into hidden burning beauty.

Art is not a class taught by Academia…
it is a holy vibration
pulsing through the veins
of those who sense the truth
of this world's perfect purity.

Art is not a transaction…
it is a soulful expression
that has no choice
but to be released
as a reflection of the Source.

Art is not a sales pitch…
it is an intense emotion
coupled with a vision
of crystalline transcendence
that ruptures open new dimensions.

Art is not yet ready for the grave…
it is a raging protest
against the mortal flesh
that sings the sweetest melody
about overcoming life's suffering.

God, Love, Truth, and Light

If you want God
I can show you to the forest
but that's a tree you'll have to find yourself

If you want Love
I can point at the moon all day
but it is the night that you'll be needing

If you want Truth
I can teach you all about addictions
but that's a drug you just can't shake

If you want Light
I can flash these shining sirens
but, sadly, most choose to fall back asleep

Coloring Outside the Lines

Blue is the color of kaleidoscope dreams
abstracted with neon mandalas
that swirl and shift
in spaces beyond
those consciousness knows how to tame.

Energy crystalized at a pressurized point
transcends the limitations
of places we fear to tread
while manifesting the miracles
that only grace can erupt into existence.

White is the color of cumulus clouds
singing hymns down from heaven
as mantras of whispered breath
hum from the lips of holy angels
to swarm across the land below.

Prophecies and prayers of old
align at the web's woven center
to reveal a matrix of truth
that boils in the heart of peace
and tears away the final veil of illusion.

Getting to Yes at All Costs

My vices lead to balance
and paradise –
without them I would be
holier than thou
on a mountain peak
caught up with myself in silent Zen.

My vices are a grounding rod
here on earth –
each sip of red wine
is a perfect reminder
of the blood
that flows through my living veins.

My virtues could be
the death of me –
trying to appease them
leaves me hollow and empty;
I cannot give
more than I have,
lest I shrivel
and shrink away
into the lonely abyss
of sainthood gone awry.

My virtues are a forced smile
on cracked desert sand –
with each blistered laugh
I lose
a little part
of what makes me human.
The dry dirt
in my mouth

dehydrates asphyxiation
down my throat.

I must have my vices
to quell the thirst –
drinking deep
and long
of this world,
I become attuned
to the vibrations of mortal flesh
where I am saved
in the pure anarchy of reason.

My virtues drive me
further away
from humanity –
into solitude and depression,
into an overload of empathy,
into compassion beyond the pale.
I cannot survive
with an open heart
that bleeds, bleeds, bleeds,
hurts, hurts, hurts
all day, all night, forever.

My vices keep me calm
and steady –
always focused on success, tapped in
to the goal, on the ready
for whatever circumstances may arise.

My vices are the Tao River –
I ride them in peace;
I flow, I flux, I catch the tide,
I surf the wave
to the shoreline

and sleep there in sublime surrender,
understanding in dreams
the dichotic nature
of my animal/angel dualism.

My virtues are the false hope
of heaven
and the ancient fear
of hell –
wrapped up in illusions
and whispered falsehoods
of mythological delusion.

My vices are the Godhead
of present moment awareness –
the absolution of Now,
the evolution of time's theory,
the progression of expansive space,
the constant high that never ceases.

My virtues are a lie,
a fakery,
a mask...the cowardice
of a yawning grave.

My vices are the dust
and ash –
the truth in all its horror,
the existential madness,
the awesomeness, the joyousness,
the suffering, the sorrow, the final acceptance,
the Great Yes to it All.

Snapshot of Eternity

The whole point
of a poem
is to capture
its moment

to give it birth
to give it breath
to give it life
to give it voice

then leave it be
to dance
to laugh
to die

Here and Now (and After)

Bury my bones
beneath the dirt
where trees once towered
before civilization took hold.

When the time comes,
let my remains
bathe naked in the soil;
no casket, no box,
no boundaries except
the caress of earth itself.

Dance and sing
atop the plot
where I'm laid to rest,
and make merry
at a funeral
filled with laughter.

But until that fateful day arrives,
let our eyes
flow with tears of joy,
let our tongues
tease out prayers of peace,
let our lips
shout words of love,
and let our lives be spent
making the most
of every moment
with which we're blessed.

Hard-Headed

Another waiting room
in another hospital
as another family member suffers
from ailments that come with old age
in America

There must be something
in the food
and water
and air
and pills
and products being pitched
on the big screen TVs

At this point
all I can think about
is how nice
the next cigarette
would be

There are still
plenty of years left
before I have to worry
about what else that will mean
down the line

If Ever There Were an Idol

Morphine drips
as a deep breath from God
to numb away your suffering
though sorrow remains

Tip of the tongue
spread from the lungs
laced through the blood
heavy on the liver
where black cells
metastasize

Deep in the mind
memories arise
of unconditional love
then
now
and forever
after

Everything good
I've learned in this life
came by observing your actions
from the very beginning

Modeling my steps
on those you took
though mine still fall short
at times

Key words
like honor
integrity

and karma
were branded
upon my consciousness
from the lessons taught
by your wise
and gentle nature

Seeking the same
in Taoist texts
Biblical scriptures
and spiritual mantras
brings a bright light
but it still pales
in comparison
to the one that shined
from your pure spirit

My Father
who art now in heaven
hallowed by thy name
in my heart
here on earth

Eulogy

The wings of ceramic angels
are too heavy now
to hold onto
or try and sculpt any longer,
no matter how beautifully
they were created in your image.

Such stone
will only weigh down the flesh,
but your spirit
is far too bountiful
and buoyant not to rise
above the gravity
of mortal life's crass concerns.

My father, your son,
is there to guide you home.
We are never truly alone,
here on earth or in heaven.
His time came far too soon,
but it now makes sense
that there needed to be a Thomas
waiting at the gates
to greet you.

I had a lucid dream last night
wherein we met and spoke.
I was able to say
all the words of gratitude
in that ethereal realm
that weren't able to be expressed
these past few years
during waking moments.

And I know
from the faith you instilled in me
that we will see each other again
in a space beyond this physical plane
where consciousness
no longer needs to communicate
using simple words
because it sings naturally
in a transcendent language
of eternal vibration.

The waterfall near the lake
where you once lived
is overflowing today
with splashing waves
of holy grace.
We all raise our glasses
to the sun
because yours is a light
that can never be depleted.
Although the world is a little dimmer now,
all the love
you left behind
in those whose lives you touched
throughout your 96 years
will shine brighter
from this day forward
to insure the illumination
of your presence
never fades.

Florence is not just a spot
marked on the map of Italy,
it is a sacred space
inscribed inside
the moral compass of our hearts.

A rose is just a rose,
but your name is a song
that we will celebrate
as if in the ballroom
where you dared to dance
with so much style and zeal.

I wake up each new morning,
open wide my eyes,
and see the seashell art
of a boat
beside my bed
that you brought back from China
after one of your journeys
across the sea.
It reminds me
that I have yet
to truly set sail
using the wind
that you blew
as a gentle breath
of guiding force
behind my back.
When I do finally visit
the vast shores
of this magical globe,
I will always remember
to carry your passion
within my blood
so that your presence
can continue burning hot
within these veins.

The greatest advice
you ever gave me
was to end each evening

by saying three things
for which I am thankful.
Thus:
I am thankful for good family.
I am thankful for good friends.
I am thankful, most of all
in this moment,
that your suffering
has been alleviated,
that your soul
has now ascended,
and that your memory
will remain forever vital
in the thoughts of those
who carry on now in your honor.

Carried Away by the Wind

And then the air
left both my lungs
as I gasped
for the breath
that no longer cared
to be held
so close,
but wanted release
toward a freedom
I couldn't fathom
beyond broken spaces
in my chest
where the organ
played its final song
called collapse.

Turn, Turn, Turn

This is not a poem
but a simple reminder
that all of these experiences
are temporary
and fleeting,
yet still
far more beautiful
than any fallen human being
could ever ask, hope,
or dare dream of.

Like a cat fight
by an oak tree
under the blanket of midnight.

Like a last kiss
on a bridge stained
with the smell of smoke.

Like a first breath
from two fresh lungs
inhaling accidental evolution.

Everyone has a breaking point.

The trick
is to come away
at the end of the process
with even more
pieces of the puzzle
in place
than there were
to begin with.

Across the Pond

London lights
flash neon blue
emblazoned
with the phoenix
in Piccadilly Circus
where energy is manic
and creativity burns
straight through the heart
of a city without fog…
if only for one night

Every language
becomes crystal clear
in a melting pot
where mussels are served
with fish and chips
and wine
and wine
and wine
that flows
along the River Thames
with accents from regions
both near and far…
if only for one night

Voices from the crowd
surface upon the stage
of The Poetry Café
where society converges
around the comforting caress
of art that slips
carefully off
the tips of tongues

teasing the promise
of renaissance
in a culture renewed...
if only for one night

Gained in Translation

Suit and tie
bluesy jazz
burns bone deep
from center stage
in Toronto.

There is no use trying to talk
or get a word in edgewise
in this deafening den of fire and light.

The music
speaks a language
of its own
with an essence
that always
matters most.

The owner behind the bar
reminds me of a woman from Albania
that used to lie, "I love you,"
every evening
before we fell asleep
(Te dua shume).

The cocktail she brings
to our flimsy table
reminds me that true love
is still just one sip away
if you drink deeply
of life
without a chaser.

There will be poetry tomorrow.
There will be a stage of our own.
There will be a scene set in motion.
But for the moment
all the movement
is humming from a guitar
that learned how to weep
with the power of gentle chaos.

Drop It Like It's Hot (Topics)

Here is my climate,
changing by the moment,
swirling around a red center,
ready for release…

Little slivers
of Lucy's diamonds
started spilling
all over the floor
into puddles
stained with blood.

Shipped across the sea
seven days a week
to fleece the fools
on every front.

You can have all the jewels back
to bathe in blood,
along with (most of) your greed.

I just want a million … or two … (for now).

This is
the most sacred moment,
resting between
the beats of your heart
after the lungs
have already expired.

Let me see you smile
(this is me begging)
one last time

(and pleading)
so I can remember you
(and praying)
three years later
(and screaming)
as the same man
(and howling)
that I knew all that time before
(at the sun/as your son).

The future has come
whether you're ready or not,
firing at will,
regardless of God's wishes.

Humanity,
in all its infinite wisdom,
freely decided long ago
to burn
this building down.

That's why we're here,
carrying a pail of water,
as the new age cycles
with a promise of peace on earth
(for those who truly seek it).

Monkeys on Mute

Here is a poem with its eyes cut out,
bound in darkness,
blinded by ignorance,
branded with a mark on its forehead
that would make Cain
toss and turn in his grave
from disbelief.

Here is a chest with a hole in its center,
bled out from the empty cavity,
hollow in the bones,
ribs picked clean
and sold to the vultures
that lurk greedily
with lust dancing
through their wicked little thoughts
of carnage.

Here is a song that haunts my soul,
just released,
spun fifty times on repeat
to reflect Revelation
as silenced ghosts from the past
materialize on the scene anew,
weeping and wailing
along with the sounds of devastation
while they linger
to cast aspersions
on all of the love
that went so wrong.

Here is a tree cracking in its trunk,
swaying in the wind,
snapping as the storm
splinters its spine to shatter
rings of ancient wisdom
that have grown burdened
from too many years
of trying to hold up the weight,
finally toppling at the highest peak
as the crown crashes
to the floor of the forest
with a thud
resounding in reverberations
felt throughout
an empire fallen.

Here is a sign screaming from the sun,
bursting with beams of black light,
boiling the oceans,
burning the fields,
breaching the contract
between heaven and earth,
unseen, unheard, unspoken,
left now to wallow
in the wastelands,
left now to pick up
the pieces
again.

Arrested Development

I saw seven dragons
with sorrow in their eyes
breathing fire from the sky
upon each other's kingdoms.
Rivers of blood
engulfed by inferno.
Scorched earth.
Hell raised.
Pillars of salt toppled
unto annihilation.
No tears for the traitors.
Wolves, defanged,
fall silent.

I saw the tantrums
screeched from a child
reach fever pitch
in a manic moment
of blackout
that left an empire in ruins.
No whitewash
on such a wicked report
could cleanse
the original sin.
The Akashic records
spell out the wasted scene
on scrolls that tip
the scales of karma
toward a type of bad mojo
that can never be recovered from.

I saw the madness of Loki
on full display
as his plans went awry;
best laid, but wound up wasted
to rot with the mice
in the trap he devised
that became
his own spoiled grave
in the end.
Six feet below
where all cries for hope
and salvation
are eternally forsaken.
There is no growth
in arid soil
for a seed
that was born diseased
with a fate
of doom
toward which it was
always destined.

Golden Oldies (Still Shimmer and Shine)

All I want is the truth,
it has been said
a time or two.

But sometimes in life
we get fed
a steady stream of lies;
it's no surprise,
and three open eyes
can always see
straight through such deception
right from the start.

All you need is love,
a certain song once harmonized
through melodic la-la-la.

But sometimes it simply is not so,
and amore
can be reduced to ash
quite fast
if it is in fact
only lust
providing the core
from which it is born.

I am the walrus.
I am the bloodhound.
I am the lucid dream awakened.
I am the vinyl record playing.

Spin the black circle
as wisdom from the past
manifests in the present
to clear our path toward the future.

Ancient proverbs
taste like promises
of righteous revolution
on the tips
of wanton tongues
that have developed a taste
for renaissance and ascension.

It will all, one day,
be dust in the wind, no doubt,
but that should never stop us now
from the screams and shouts
that rock and roll
our heavy metal momentum
toward dance hall bliss
imbibed in double doses
and imbued
with the graceful glory
of a starlit
symphonic concert.

We are the cosmos.
We are the night owl.
We are the seat of the soul.
We are the story as it unfolds.
Coo coo cachoo.

Igniting Intention

The only hell in life
I could possibly imagine
would come from squandering
the gift of light
that pulses within my soul.

Poetry is just a language I use
to fallibly express
the ineffable emotions
that long to be birthed into form,
and so I know for sure
that the written word
is but a single spoke
on the much larger wheel of action
that can only be turned
by forever placing
one foot in front of the next.

You don't always
have to bust through a wall
when there are other routes open
over and around it
that can more easily be accessed
by using the wisdom gained
from lessons learned in the past.

Constant, continual, progressive,
evolutionary
movement forward
is the holy key to unlock
the gates of heaven
here on earth.

Mind, body, and spirit
triangulate the vision
when three eyes become focused
on the destiny
that finally arrives
once fate and freewill
have been balanced
into a perfect rhythm
of harmony and accord.

This is not a prayer,
but a promise.

This is not a hope,
but a hallelujah.

This is not a dream,
but an awakening.

This is not a posture,
but a privilege.

This is not a choice,
but an acceptance.

Cometh the Key

September crawls inside my chest,
burrows its head
like an ostrich
turning eggs within the heart.
Cracks a few
in the parts that were almost stolen
to cook an omelet
and resurrect the flesh
until the beat is synchronized again
in a healthy rhythm.

The day of birth is both brutal and bloody.
The womb of God
is an ocean of pleasure,
but the suffering experienced on earth
balances out the equation in full.

Each of us will learn
in due time
how righteously
the scales truly operate.
Rip out your feathers
and paint them gold.
The silver rule is a war cry
from eagles perched on high,
waiting patiently,
ready to swoop
at the first sign of weakness.
Survival of the fittest
means you best become wise
to the ways
of this wicked world's nature.

The only sin
is not standing back up.
Take ten strokes
and rise again
with the holy ghost
of your own forgiveness.
Double the dose of eleven
to find salvation
in one tick of the clock
that holds its breath
until eternity ignites.

Veins are a river of fire,
bones are the trunk of a tree,
saliva drips from a tongue
wanton with lust
in the sacred spots
that gently coax sweet sighs.
Milk and honey
between wet thighs of revelation
open the gateway to revolution.
Taste of old wine
until its skin grows sour,
but then drink deeply from the cup
that offers new power.
How many licks does it take
to get to the core
in the kingdom of heaven?
The look as her eyes
roll back
provides the key.

Faith Buried in the Soil

This is the spot
where the sun went down
on our season.
Laid to rest
with a blanket of feathers
to cover the scene.
There is no flight
once wings
become trapped beneath ice.

I can feel the chilled
winds of October
sweep across
my cold, brittle bones.
The marrow is frozen
like your love
stopped on a dime...
and then died.
But not mine.
It took time
for that open wound
to finally heal.

Hours move forward
at the speed of sap
spilling from an aged trunk
where initials
carved in the shape of a heart
sew themselves shut
to symbolize
the signature of separation.

We each walk
our own path through life
with intentions to never betray,
but sometimes star-crossed lines
only intersect for a brief
moment in time
before splitting and going astray.
What was once parallel
in synchronized form
grew more obtuse
with each step taken
at an outward angle
behind my back.
Three stabs
from your knife
followed by a slash
to inflict the gash
of harshest measure.

The pressure valve
of steam is released
in this new moment.
A melting point reached
here with the trees
as autumn leaves
fall colorfully to the ground.
Planting a seed
for the coming spring
because each turn,
good or bad,
deserves another.

Hymns from the Choir

My heart is a crystal
reflecting the light
of a thousand generations,
stored as a prismatic shard
in the center
of ancestral DNA's
raging fire.

So you can suck it
from my chest,
chew it up,
spit it out,
and stomp it into the dirt
with both feet,
but each new night
when I fall asleep
sweet dreams of grace
will call forth its resurrection
come morning sun.

I turn the other cheek
to the madness of this world
and kiss the stars
hanging above France
with an electric tongue
that hums
as the holy taste
of hallelujah
tickles each bud
with a touch of inspiration.

The consciousness of Christ
married Buddha's precepts
in my mind,
and now visions of Tao align
to keep me safe
during every windswept
bending of the willow.

The trees are bursting
with autumn hues
as bright colors sing
Psalms of forgiveness
throughout the forest,
and birds above
join in the chorus
to transform this space
into a church
of sacred rhythms.

A million miles
are still stretched out
upon the path of life's journey
before me,
but the present moment
here and now
feels just like home,
and so every step
is filled with love
toward a future
coated with the comfort
of salvation's warmth.

Crown Jewel

Sun-kissed
upon my temple
from the rays
of a clear blue sky
in late October,
warming hopeful flesh
while cold air
breathes crisp and calm.

I will never claim
to be a saint,
but I have walked a path
away from sin
and now worship
at the altar
of a halo
that shines serenely
with a holy radiance
of light
both pure and pristine.

Water infused
with minerals
from an ancient sea
douses my blood
as a fire reignites
to salt every cell
with an energetic charge
that hums electric verses
until the synchronized
bird song
joining along
from lofty branches above

becomes a crystallized note
piercing through the wind.

Sitting silently still
upon a park bench
as my thoughts dance
along with the rhythm
stirred by leaves
shaking on tress
as their vibrant colors
emerge
in autumn hues
of an erupting
righteous palette.

Orange is the shade
of angel wings
distilled in an amber moment
while yellow intentions
shoot up and down the spine
to align
as a sanctified sign
that green heart chakras
are set to burst
in a frenzied flurry
of awakened harmonics.

Consciousness implodes,
careening inwardly,
before flowing back outward
in tune
with a gentle breeze
that frees
darkly frozen shadows
from hidden spaces,
melting their essence

under a brilliant orb
burning brightly
toward a future
birthed clean
with the absolution of faith
after our fall
has been officially weathered.

Collection Agency of Chaos

I want to lick
the open wound
of November
and taste
its gushing blood
as it drains
from a sieve
through the sky
to the tip
of my tongue
with a lustful tease
of what's still to come.

All the suffering
and sorrow
of a society gone mad
is one quick fix
pill away
from being swallowed
as a hair-trigger solution
toward faux salvation
on the empty stomach
of a collective system.

So buy, buy, buy
the terrible lies
that help to line
their sleazy pockets
with a fresh
pound of flesh;
I'll cut it myself
from out our chest
and send it

with a kiss
across the sea
where a singing siren
dances atop rocks
designed to crash
with a lure
of deceptive comfort.

I want to topple
the tower
of flashing lights
and smash
its windows of glass
to the ground
where they splinter
into shards
that slice through veins,
flooding the concoction
of a cursed
chemical cocktail
that flows freely
to the core
of final corruption.

So numb, numb, numb
your consciousness
with a twist of fate
served to order
on a silver platter,
and then wait
for golden feathers
to be weighed
on a rigged scale
when karma comes calling
for its overdue fines
of damnation.

Sapling (Fuzzy Math)

I am not a poet;
it's just a thing I do
while trying to figure out
how to fix
this life I failed
on the first go round.

I am just a man
seeking to learn from my mistakes
so I can make the most of second chances
for the millionth time.

If Not Now...

I seek to shine in spite of my darkness.
In fact, it was a kiss of death
that forced me to fully embrace the light.

At the end of a rope
there is but one question
that truly matters:
how strong is your grip?

I burn because my blood and bones are kerosene.
After the fire, it was a barren field of ash
that showed me where to plant new seeds of life.

When surfacing for air
there is a certain thought
that takes precedence over all others:
are you still breathing?

I always try to fight my wars from a firm footing of peace.
Within the schism, it was a mirror of nature
that birthed the bite of our dualistic tongue.

As the sun sets below
that horizon in the distance
there remains only this to ask:
will we rise again tomorrow?

Divorced from Self/Born Anew

One of the least enjoyable
experiences in life
is having one's ego crushed,
but God knows
it may also just
turn out to be
the most important
in the end.

For better
or for worse.

ON THE ROAD, HEATED AND SEARCHING
FOR HYDRATION, WHILE DREAMING OF A
SKY-BLUE FUTURE WITH POISON-GREEN HANGOVERS
PASSING BY SEASICK HIGHWAYS AND GREY PASSENGERS
THE COLOR OF LIFE WILL INSPIRE US FOR A RANCID
WORK OF ART THE SOOTHING HEAT MELTS MY BRAIN.

TO A JOYFULL MUSH AND EVEN IF I'M EATING
KILOMETERS WITHOUT HUNGER FOR CIVILIZATION
FLEEING FOR THE UNDERGROUND, THAT WHAT
THE MAP JUST DOESN'T SHOW, LOOKING AT A
DISTANCE AT OUR BEAUTIFUL SHITTY SYSTEM,
WE'LL KEEP LAUGHING, HANGING,
DRIVING, DUMB, YOUNG AND
NEVER ALONE

It's a Matter of Record/Opinion

Tell me something meaningful
and make sure I believe it
before you double down my debts.

Then dance in your pride and vanity.
Then dance in your ignorance and vanity.
Then dance in your shaken identity.
Then dance, then dance, then dance
in vanity.

Pat yourself on the back, pat me on the back,
pat myself on the back, pat you on the back,
pat us on the back, pat we on the back,
pat them on the back, I take it all back,
I take it all…

thin air, thin air, thin air…

There are ghosts in the system,
ghosts in the visions,
ghosts in the world,
ghosts in your pores,
ghosts pouring out…

Smoke in your eyes, smoke in your hair,
smoke on your tongue, fire in your lungs,
fire in your heart, fire, fire, fire…

always burns…

thin ice, thin ice, thin ice…

All your sins have been collected
from a life you didn't live
so pray to the gods of Big Data
and confess that your days have been numbered
drifting through the endless stream,
scrolling through the timelines of life,
searching for the source to find connection.

Tell me something meaningful
in every single moment
and make sure I buy, buy, buy
but never sell...

out and down, down and out...

never doubt, never doubt, never doubt
that there is destiny
and there is dust in the...

thin air, thin air, thin air...

There are seeds in the ground,
there is blood in the roots,
there is will in the shoots,
there is power in the bloom.

Extinction Is the Genesis of Evolution

Crossing the bridge from distortion into silence
creates the electric hum of a new awakening.
If art is an unfolding rhythm
then life must be a song in motion.
There are certain comparisons that never seem
to pop up on any quizzes or SAT questions in class.

I will grade true love on a scale of forgiveness.
I will slide with a smile
until slipping through the veil of illusions.
I will spit in the river and witness all ripples.

Burning a drag of smoke with no filter
enlivens the flesh of wet lungs to breathe fresh oxygen.
If the bond is stronger than blood
then first kisses are a quickening.
Squirrels naturally seek after fallen nuts near the tree
as deeply the mind digs its roots in for winter.

I will promise you less until the future delivers.
I will dance on this spot as the soil grows richer.
I will lick morning dew from the blades of your grass.

Watching leaves wither toward their inevitable extinction
pushes evolution's theory to renew its efforts with vigor.
If God is but a dream
then I'm happy now to slumber in peace.
Visions carry more weight with the yawning stars
when constellations crystalize in manifested hearts.

I will cherish your eyes when the sun hangs in solstice.
I will hold both your hands when the waves crash upon us.
I will never release from time's wings as they flutter.

Sex and Death

The eyes
roll toward heaven
either way

Cavity

If you whisper into the night
the hounds will hear you
the owls will hear you
the old gods will hear you
the ghosts will hear you
the gravesites will hear you
the future will hear you

Coughing up triangles
in your doublespeak
It's three over two
and our theory is restless

Seven layers of lung
Eleven beams of light
Thirteen brands of chaos

Wisdom tooth pulled in innocence
left us wanting for the right verbs
Go back and call it a fit
of ignorance

If you scream into the void
If you laugh into the void
you will hear an echo

Portals

Stars are holes
in the sky
bleeding through heaven's veil

I would swallow the light

I would choke on the hemlock
if I thought it might
bring you back
down to earth

I stare at the moon
every 28th day
and pray
that we survive another cycle

I watched you digest their poison

I watched you drink deep
with faith in their bombs
from the soothing lull
of that siren song

Chew on the edges of night
to taste the angle
where source floods
the shape of flesh

Your yawn could birth a universe

Your sigh could shake foundations
to the core

Tender Loving

I want to rip the ghosts from your eyes,
breathe them deep into my lungs,
and bury them at my own core
so you can sleep in peace at night
without hearing all their haunting wails.

I want to tease out the secrets
hiding behind your broken smile
so they can dance across your lips
to mute the need for silence
and bless your swollen heart to sing.

I want to divorce your fear
from the darkness
and shine wicked lights of truth
on the spots that hurt the most
so the wounds will finally heal.

I want to pull the knife from your back
using sharpened claws and fangs
and lick to clean the open gash
with a peroxide-laced tongue
and bloody rags doused in sweat.

I want to suck the snake-oil from your neck,
swallow the medicine,
spit out the venom,
and beg the poison to burn away
so ash can feed the flowers of trust.

I want to show you to the fields of chaos
where you can witness their work at play
as bombs descend with eerie whispers

upon a body waiting for acts of war
to trigger all its survival instincts.

I want to lose my mind in yours a while
to watch the notes rise and fall
and learn the sound madness makes
in the moment before the waves break
and your raft of peace is sent back to shore.

Crystal Balls and Uncaged Birds

I will not call you a Goddess
I will not claim you're an angel
I will not charge you as being a muse

I will not put you on a pedestal
I will not worship you
I will not idolize you

because this life
is not a poem
but art in motion

I will not call this heaven on earth
when all that truly matters is love in the heart

I will not waste all our time with words
when it's more important to laugh and dance

I will not call you a Goddess
but I will believe it just the same

I will not claim you have wings
but I will watch your back
and walk by your side
here on the ground for all of our days

Tied Together

I need a centerpiece
to capture my heart
and build a home there

I need a love
that expands beyond
alpha and omega

I need a partner
that sees past my faults
and helps to heal them

I need a goddess
to cast spells
that last a lifetime

I need a trust
that takes each leap
with faith in tow

I need a warrior
prepared to fight
to keep the peace

I need a truth
that has no choice
but to shine with honor

I need a you
in this moment
for all eternity

Eye to Eye

I have searched for Truth
and found it lacking
in this wicked world
full of falsehoods
as liars
lead their brethren
toward the edge of despair.

I have searched for Peace
amongst the many tribes
across all lands
where nature remains pure
even as manufactured wars
are brought to a crescendo
of madness and chaotic turbulence.

I have searched for Empathy
with empty palms
while sand drains
through the clenched fists
of would-be conquerors
who use faked compassion
as a means to distort consciousness.

I have searched for Love
and finally learned the lesson
that such an emotion
must first be discovered within one's own soul
before it can ever be
realized in the eyes of another
who values their self on the same level.

Vines

Vines attach
their grip
while continuing to
expand in proportion

just as my heart
is set in place
with you
yet still growing

only so
I can learn
how to love you
even more

Prometheus Should Have Doubled down for More

Sitting here
where the sky falls,
where the rain pours,
where the gods weep,
where the season shifts,
where the air growls,
where electric wonder
becomes second nature,
I can only smile
as my spine shivers
from a kundalini force
that packs a punch.

Breathe into me
with your sacred whisper
as my bones shake,
as my flesh sighs,
as my blood churns,
as my hope soars,
as my dreams scream,
as my heart opens
to the sound of your voice,
and I will promise
eternity and more
even if I must steal time
straight from the source.

Natural Reflection of Your Palms

This is my breath, the same as yours,
the same as dust, the same as ash
when it all comes to an end,
but held deeply within
steady lungs
that long for truth
while we're still here.

This is my flesh, the same as yours,
the same as tissue, the same as sinew,
but without
fiber optic connections as of now;
and never will be,
so don't dare try me
with temptations
toward such so-called system upgrades.

This is my blood, the same as yours,
the same as a river, the same as the ocean
where we all swam
before the expansion
of our evolution
was set into forward motion.

These are my hands, the same as yours,
the same as caring, the same as giving,
the same as taking, the same as wanting,
the same as needing to hold
everything that is loved
firmly within their grasp.

Rhyme and Reason

Is that hawk screaming
about whether or not
it believes in the existence of God?

Or simply seeking
across the distance
with a signal for its lover?

Is that blade of grass
straining against gravity
to grow taller toward the sky?

Or allowing its roots
below the ground
to do their business behind the scenes?

Is that cloud concerned
about bunkers being built
in fear of bombs?

Or being carried carefree
by a gentle breeze
blowing through the air?

Is that star all bent out of shape
over the latest debate
raging on cable news?

Or shining as a beacon of light
to more galaxies
than can be fathomed?

Is that leaf throwing a fit
about cold weather
as the season begins to shift?

Or brightening the woods
with a brilliant autumn hue
before falling back to the soil?

Is that wave cursing at the moon
about the way in which
it's made to move?

Or crashing upon the shore
with a splash to fulfill
its natural fate of ebb and flow?

A Time to Seek

There will not always be happiness in life,
and despite what any yogi, guru, or spiritual master
might profess,
there will be times of stress, suffering, sadness,
and sorrow;
so it goes.

But there can be cultivated
a place of perfect peace
in the inward spaces
of the heart, mind, and spirit;
and so,
no matter how
the sky may storm
or the waters rage,
there will remain
a safe haven of shelter
to offer solace.

Seek always
the Kingdom of God found within,
and you just might begin
to understand
with deeper wisdom
how you are being delivered
everything you need
in each moment
to evolve.

Theory of Evolution

Not every step in life
is meant to be smooth;
how else could we grow
and learn along the path?

Not every word from our mouths
can come out perfectly clean;
how else could we be pushed
to expand our language of love?

Not every truth that they claim to have
is quite so self-evident and clear;
how else could these documents breathe
and bring about a more peaceful union?

Not every glimmer in our eyes
is meant to sparkle with the stars;
how else could we seek God
in moments of silent darkness?

Not every song from the birds
can lead to a symphony under the sun;
how else could the hawks soaring the sky
find a feast to keep their wings strong?

Not every moment in time
can be blessed by the divine…
or maybe that's wrong,
because I swear
that with you by my side
it all seems holy.

Press Any Button

Thompson said:
Buy the ticket, take the ride.

The only subtle alteration I would make
is that admission to the party
always remains free
for those who truly came to dance.

Also, there is no way off (or out)
once the ignition switch has been hit…
which isn't a bad thing at all
so long as you're careful around the curves.

Saucy Salvation

Jesus preached
to turn the other cheek,
but he also had a thing for whips.

All I know
is that these mixed messages
are awfully kinky,
and so I'm not quite sure
whether we should hit the sack
or start slashing
every banker's bag of silver.

Heart-Shaped Phoenix

Cobain quoted Young by writing:
It's better to burn out
than to fade away.

I would humbly suggest
that there is still plenty
of gasoline to go around…
so we can dance
around these flames
for quite awhile
before our little hearts
have had their fill
of fiery fun.

Looking for a Cherry

Vonnegut wrote:
So it goes.

So it did,
so it does,
so it ever will.

I suppose some truths
just can't be topped.

Voyaging Inward

Lao Tzu stated
that a journey of 1,000 miles
begins with a single step.

Well, I passed that marker ages ago,
and my shoes might be full of holes
but my feet have become tough as nails.

The things of this world
are mortal and fleeting,
but the presence of God
is always one heartbeat away.

Wheels in Motion

I have loved in life the same as you,
won and lost that hand a time or two,
but never cursed the way that cards were dealt,
never blamed the course of shooting stars,
never bet my luck on pennies falling from the sky,
never begged for more or less than what is fair.

I have watched ancient cities crumble across the screen,
laughed and wept in madness at burning dreams,
but never thought my faith was not enough,
never went to war without just cause,
never blinded eyes to spite the heart,
never doubted fate would play its part.

I have seen the way this world turns,
been told time and again we live and learn,
but never cast aspersions at holy angels,
never damned the demons for their nature,
never stole red fire from the sun,
never lusted after glory that wasn't won.

I have stumbled through darkness the same as you,
battled my own shadows seeking truth,
but never pointed fingers at the moon,
never raged at light when nights went black,
never bartered my good soul when I fell down,
never failed to stand back up on solid ground.

Ace in the Hole

Enlightenment
is the grass stain
on your white pants
when you fall hard
but come to find
that you landed
in a fresh patch
of lucky clovers.

Paint me every angle
of evolution
in a spectrum
of green
more electric
than what these
weary eyes
have seen.

Awareness
is the kick
in your throat
when you learn
how to choke
and cough up
black cancer
in waves.

Sing to me
across
the seven seas
in triple threes
as blue aces
rise with a roaring tide.

Consciousness
is the final sip
of clean water
when the desert mirage
vanishes
beneath the sand
but forces your hand
toward a fast
that leads to light
saving your soul
in the end.

Walk with me in spirit
beyond this arid wasteland
until all the colors
of creation
have been burnt
into my psyche.

Epiphany
is the sound
of dreams
shattering
from stones
thrown
straight through
stained glass
to collapse
the last
wink of sleep
and awaken
the feast
of a new reality
being manifested
into form.

Teach me the prayer
of well-weathered truth
that I can whisper
with peace
when the winds begin to blow.

Better Take a Big One

I felt you blink
in the eye of the storm
as Atlantis went under

There was nothing left
for us to do
but breathe

sigh

and rise

again

Trembling toward the Sun

How much distance and difference is there
between a mountain and a molehill?

And how far are you determined to climb
to insure your problems amount to blessings in the end?

How tenacious is your will to peace?
How deep is your reservoir of faith?

When you weep with me
do so not out of sorrow
but exultation
and know that even in our suffering
there shines a light of salvation.

How many skeletons are there living in your closet
that rattle bones when you can't sleep at night?

And how tired are the dragons that guard the secrets
hiding in the shadows that haunt your soul?

How dedicated is your tongue to truth?
How strong is your resolve in the fire?

When you dance with me
do so not in half steps
but full measure
and know that every movement
guides us closer to the stars.

How many millstones hang around your neck
as you drag your cross from earth to sea to sky?

And how many psalms do you recite in darkness
as a prayer for healing to arrive with dawn?

How inspired is your passion?
How embedded is your urge to ascend?

When you sing with me
do so not in low key
but high spirits
and know that this language of lyrics
is born of revival.

Acknowledgements

"Transcending Definitions"; "Carried Away by the Wind"; "Turn, Turn, Turn"; "Drop It Like It's Hot (Topics); Golden Oldies (Still Shimmer and Shine)"; Igniting Intention"; "Collection Agency of Chaos"; "Divorced from Self/Born Anew"; "It's a Matter of Record/Opinion"; "Cavity"; "Portals"; and "Better Take a Big One" were originally published in Dissident Voice.

"God, Love, Truth, and Light"; and "Monkeys on Mute" were originally published in Eunoia Review.

"Coloring Outside the Lines"; and "Here and Now (and After) were originally published in Tuck Magazine.

"Getting to Yes at All Costs" was originally published in Sentinel Literary Quarterly.

"Snapshot of Eternity" was originally published in Ink in Thirds.

"Hard-Headed" was originally published in the 2017 Peeking Cat Poetry Magazine Anthology.

"If Ever There Were an Idol" was originally published in The Galway Review.

"Across the Pond" was originally published in the 2018 Atunis Galaxy Anthology.

"Gained in Translation" was originally published in Lummox Press Anthology.

"Cometh the Key" was originally published in Eos: The Creative Context.

"If Not Now…" was originally published in Episteme Journal.

"Extinction is the Genesis of Evolution" was originally published in 1932 Quarterly.

"Sex and Death" was originally published in Ethos Literary Journal.

"Tender Loving" was originally published in Poetry and Creativity.

"Tied Together" was originally published in Ariel Chart.

"Eye to Eye" was originally published in New Ink Review.

"Vines" was originally published in The Pangolin Review.

"Prometheus Should Have Doubled down for More" was originally published in Poetry Poetics Pleasure Ezine.

"Natural Reflection of Your Palms" was originally published in Leaves of the Poet Tree.

"Rhyme and Reason" was originally published in Medusa's Kitchen.

"A Time to Seek" was originally published in The Beautiful Space.

"Theory of Evolution" was originally published in Harbinger Asylum.

"Saucy Salvation" was originally published in Yellow Chair Review.

"Heart-Shaped Phoenix"; and "Looking for a Cherry" were originally published in Venus in Scorpio Zine.

"Voyaging Inward" was originally published in Leaves of Ink.

"Wheels in Motion" was originally published in The Poet's Attic Anthology.

"Ace in the Hole" was originally published in Mahatma Guru.

"Trembling toward the Sun" was originally published in the Essential Existentialism Anthology from Creative Talents Unleashed.

ALSO AVAILABLE FROM ALIEN BUDDHA PRESS

Mar-a-Lago Teetotaler by Maxwell Ryder

The Art of Changing Nothing to Punk Gigs by Sudeep Adhikari

Vegas Poems by Ryan Quinn Flanagan

Frenetic/No Contest by Dustin Pickering

Winds of Time by JoyAnne O'Donnell

Alien Buddha Cums to Jesus by Jay Miner and Jeff Flipski

Dimensional High by Ammi Romero

Poison in Paradise by Scott Thomas Outlar

LOCOmotion of Life by Adam Levon Brown

Screamo Lullabies by Robert J.W

Surfing the Appalachian Vortex by Mark Hartenbach

Irritable Brain Syndrome by Willie Smith

About Consciousness by Heath Brougher

Heroin by Catfish McDaris

36 Haikus and a Horror Story by Red Focks

Death to Fairy Tales by Alex S. Johnson

Deathbed Colored Glasses by Rob Plath

A Stab in the Dark by Bengt O Björklund

Adventures in Space and Other Selected Casualties by Richard D. Houff

Words Whispered and Screamed Over the Great Lakes by Jeremy Stolz

Duffy Street & Other Dubious Incidents by Red Focks

Death is Not Our Holy Word by Adam Levon Brown

Tweak Vision by Andrew Darlington

Madhouse by Honcho Mars

Sleeping With Wildflowers by Elancharan Gunasekaran

Some Little Pricks by R. Keith

This Space Between Us by Gabriel Bates

God's Breath by Stefan Bohdan

The Northern Sunset by Steven Storrie

My Reality by Matt Borczon

Losing a Balloon by Billy Antonio

Broken Branches by Thasia Anne

A Ludicrous Split by Kevin Ridgeway and Gabriel Ricard

Little Hollywood by Luke Kuzmish

It's Colder Than Hell/ Starving Elves Eat Reindeer Meat/ Santa Claus is Dead by Jeff Weddle

The Diablo's Pistolas by Stefan Bohdan

God's Silence a Lion's Roar by Stefan Bohdan

This Useless Beauty by Jason Baldinger

Home Memories by Gideon Cecil

Return to Vegas Poems by Ryan Quinn Flanagan

Dusty Video Game Cartridges by Robert J.W.

Somebody's Book of the Dead by Mark Borczon

Bastard of a Poet by Leah Mueller

Zugzwang by R. Keith

Poetry Is: A Dirty Word by Richard J Cronborg

The House by Heidi Blakeslee

Belly Laughs by Chelsea Bergeron

No One Approves Of My Methods by Clinton J. Ruttan

The Black and the Blues by Jay Passer

Mannequin Legs & Other Tales by Robert Ragan

Philosopher's Ship by John Grochalski

Crashing the Zen Piñata by Mark Hartenbach

Howl Drunkenly at the Moon by Nathan Tompkins

Freud's Haberdashery Habit by Mike Fiorito

(Pseudonym Lastname #1) Anime Fight Battle: Japan by Red Focks and Ammi

Cave Dreams to Star Portals by Chani Zwibel

In Which The World is Turned Upside Down: & an idiot is running the country by Thomas R. Thomas

84028744R00062

Made in the USA
San Bernardino, CA
02 August 2018